CCSS Genre Drama

Essential Question
When are decisions hard to make?

The Missing Swimsuit

by Hugh Brown • illustrated by Reggie Holladay

Act 1
Strange Happenings. 2

Act 2
She's No Angel 9

Act 3
Solving the Case. 13

Respond to Reading 16

PAIRED READ Movies: Plays on Film? 17

Focus on Genre 20

Act 1
Strange Happenings

Characters:
LISA

TYRONE (Lisa's brother)

CARA (Lisa and Tyrone's friend and Jett's sister)

JETT (Lisa and Tyrone's friend and Cara's brother)

ANGEL (a new girl at school)

COACH JAMESON (swim coach)

MOM (Lisa and Tyrone's mother)

Scene 1

Scene: *A school cafeteria*

LISA, TYRONE, CARA, and JETT are sitting with their lunch trays in front of them.

CARA: (*talking to LISA and gesturing to her own lunch tray*) Say my tray is the swimming pool.

TYRONE: My tray is the swimming pool.

CARA: (*ignoring him*) My tray is the swimming pool, and these are the swimmers at your race next week.

She arranges pieces of fruit along one end of the tray.

CARA: Here's how the race is going to go.

She moves the apple to the other end of the tray.

LISA: I hope I was the apple.

CARA: Of course you were.

LISA: I'm not sure. The new girl, Angel, is pretty fast.

ANGEL *walks past.*

TYRONE: (*whispering*) Speak of the—

LISA: Hi, Angel.

ANGEL *is looking the other way and doesn't react.*

JETT: She totally ignored you!

TYRONE: (*laughing*) She looked exactly like that cat that's been hanging around our yard. You say hello, and it just twitches its tail and walks on by with its nose in the air. We should call that cat Angel.

LISA: Maybe she just didn't hear me.

Scene 2

Scene: *By the pool before practice*

CARA *is in her swimsuit.* **LISA** *rushes in, still in her school clothes.*

CARA: Why aren't you dressed? Practice is going to start any minute, and you know how grumpy Coach Jameson gets if you're late.

LISA: I can't find my swimsuit. I'm sure I put it in my bag this morning.

CARA: Maybe it fell out of your bag and someone picked it up. Was anyone else in the changing room?

LISA: Just Angel.

CARA: Well, she doesn't seem very nice, does she? Maybe she wouldn't even tell you if she saw your swimsuit.

ANGEL *approaches, also ready for swim practice. She starts to walk up to the girls and then slows when she sees* **CARA'S** *expression.*

CARA: (*slightly accusing*) Hey, have you seen Lisa's swimsuit? She can't find it.

ANGEL: No ... sorry.

She hurries away.

CARA: That was strange.

LISA: Can you blame her? You weren't being very friendly. She's new here, you know. We should try to make friends with her. We're on the same team, after all.

CARA: I guess. Do you need help finding your swimsuit?

LISA: No, that's okay. There's no reason why we should both be late. But wish me luck with Coach Jameson!

CARA: You probably don't even need it. You know you're Coach's favorite. Anyway, see you later.

LISA: Bye.

> **CARA** *walks away toward the pool as* **COACH JAMESON** *enters from the same direction.*

COACH JAMESON: What's the holdup, Lisa? Everyone else is already in the pool. Angel's already on her fifth lap.

LISA: Sorry, Coach. I can't find my swimsuit. I don't know what could have happened to it.

COACH JAMESON: (*grinning*) Are you sure that's it? I think maybe you're afraid to swim now that you have some serious competition. I think you and Angel will be good for each other. Nothing beats a little healthy competition to help people strive for their best.

LISA: (*slightly uncomfortable*) Sure. Well, I'll definitely be back tomorrow—with my swimsuit.

> **LISA** *walks away in one direction,* **COACH JAMESON** *in the other.*

Scene 3

Scene: *The school cafeteria the next day*

LISA, **TYRONE**, **CARA**, *and* **JETT** *are sitting at their table again.* **ANGEL** *is sitting alone at a nearby table.*

LISA: So one minute it's there, and the next … gone.

TYRONE: (*waving an imaginary wand*) Abracadabra … Poof! (*to* **JETT**) A mysterious tale, my dear Watson. It's up to us to solve the infamous case of the disappearing swimsuit.

JETT: (*getting into the act*) So who took it, Sherlock?

CARA: (*in a man's voice*) Elementary, my dear Watson. From my extensive experience with a multitude of similar cases, I can definitively say it was the butler.

LISA: Well, whoever it was, it was really annoying. And kind of embarrassing too. Coach asked if I'd left it behind on purpose because I was too scared to swim against Angel.

TYRONE: (*looking at* **ANGEL**) Hmmm.

LISA: Come on, people! How about a little empathy?

JETT *and* **TYRONE** *start hamming it up.*

JETT: (*in a falsetto voice*) How absolutely ghastly!

TYRONE: (*in a gruff voice*) How utterly appalling!

LISA *pretends to be offended but is smiling.*

CARA: (*still as Sherlock Holmes*) My next endeavor is to solve this mysterious case using all the skills that the task will entail.

TYRONE: I bet Angel did it. You said she was the only other person in the changing room. Maybe she took it when you were looking the other way.

LISA: But why? She couldn't wear it, or we'd all notice.

CARA: I know why—she took it so you couldn't practice before the race! She knows you're faster, and she wants to beat you any way she can.

TYRONE: We should go tell her to give it back.

CARA *stands up, as if to move over to confront* **ANGEL**.

LISA: Hey, wait a minute! Whatever happened to guilty until proven innocent?

JETT: Didn't you mean to say that the other way around?

TYRONE: (*using his arms to pretend to close a clapboard*) The Missing Swimsuit ... Take Two!

LISA: (*repeating herself as if nothing has happened*) Wait! Whatever happened to innocent until proven guilty?

CARA: Well, it's not—

> **TYRONE** shushes her as **ANGEL** walks over.

ANGEL: Hi, Lisa. Did you ever find your swimsuit?

> **CARA** and **TYRONE** stare at her suspiciously. **ANGEL** hurries off before **LISA** has the chance to reply.

LISA: Okay—so that was a little weird.

CARA: She had guilty written all over her.

TYRONE: Yeah, I'm pretty sure I saw "I took the swimsuit" stamped on her forehead.

LISA: Well, I guess it doesn't matter now. Mom bought me a new swimsuit, so I'll just concentrate on winning that race.

Act 2
She's No Angel

Scene 1

Scene: *The school cafeteria the next day*

The four friends are once again sitting at their table over lunch, with **ANGEL** *by herself at a nearby table.*

TYRONE: You'll never believe what happened. Swimsuit number two.

CARA: No way!

LISA: I left it drying on a chair on the deck last night. This morning … gone.

TYRONE: And guess who she saw running off down the road with a swimsuit in her hand?

CARA and **JETT:** (*in unison*) Angel!

TYRONE: Ding! Ten points to Cara and Jett.

LISA: I didn't actually see her with it. But I'm pretty sure I did see her walking away just past our driveway.

CARA: Then she definitely took it.

They all look over at **ANGEL**. *She smiles.*

LISA: And Mom thinks I'm just being careless. I'm sick of it. Not that I'm saying Angel absolutely, positively did it … (*voice trailing off in indecision*)

CARA: Of course she did.

JETT: Did you see that smile? She's totally gloating!

LISA: I have to admit it did look like that.

Scene 2

Scene: **LISA** *and* **TYRONE'S** *kitchen*

MOM *and* **TYRONE** *are making dinner.*

LISA: (*storming in with a laundry basket*) You won't believe it!

MOM: Try me.

LISA: It's gone! It was there, then I went next door to talk to Cara, and now it's gone.

MOM: I hope you're not talking about your second new swimsuit. That makes three you've lost.

TYRONE: (*sprinting out of the kitchen*) I'll get her!

MOM: What set him off?

LISA: He's probably trying to catch Angel.

MOM: You mean Angel Reyes from down the road?

LISA: We think she's been taking my swimsuits to keep me from training so she can beat me in the race.

MOM: Whoa ... back up, honey. Ten minutes ago, you went outside with the laundry basket. Then what?

LISA: Cara was playing with that stray cat, the one we call Angel. I put the laundry basket down and went to play with the cat, too. It ran away, then I talked to Cara for about five seconds. When I went back to hang up the clothes, my swimsuit was gone.

MOM: Have you checked all along where you walked?

LISA: Three times.

TYRONE: (*coming back into the room*) Sorry, sis. I was faster than a speeding bullet, but she was already gone.

10

11

MOM: So what's the story with Angel? The girl, not the cat.

TYRONE: She's been stealing Lisa's swimsuits.

MOM: I really don't see why you would think that. She seems like a very nice girl.

TYRONE: Ah, yes, but under that shy exterior lurks …

LISA: Tyrone! Can you be serious for one minute?

TYRONE: Sorry.

LISA: (*talking faster and faster as* **MOM** *looks more and more irritated*) The first time my swimsuit disappeared, she was the only one in the changing room. The second time, I'm pretty sure I saw her down by our driveway, and she's been acting really weird at school, and if I didn't swim, she'd definitely win because … (*pauses for breath*)

MOM: That sounds like a whole lot of flimsy circumstantial evidence to cover up your own carelessness. I'm sure Angel is a nice girl. You should give her the benefit of the doubt.

TYRONE: Guilty until proven innocent.

LISA *frowns at him, but* **MOM** *hasn't noticed he's said it wrong.*

MOM: Exactly. You have to be more careful with your belongings. Unless you can find a benefactor to supply you with limitless swimsuits, you'll have to start paying for them yourself.

MOM *walks out, and* **LISA** *sits down in a huff.*

Act 3
Solving the Case

Scene 1

Scene: *By the swimming pool on race day*

LISA, **TYRONE**, **CARA**, *and* **JETT** *are celebrating* **LISA'S** *victory.*

LISA: (*grinning*) I'm glad that's over.

CARA: (*gleefully*) You beat you-know-who hands down.

LISA: Not by that much, actually.

JETT: It was enough.

TYRONE: It was huge!

ANGEL: (*walking up and smiling tentatively*) Congratulations! You swam really well. I'm really glad that you swam. It wouldn't have been any fun to win just because you weren't in the race.

LISA: Thanks. You had a really good race, too.

ANGEL: Thanks. Well, see you around. (*She leaves.*)

LISA: I really don't think she did it. It doesn't make sense if she wanted me to race.

CARA: (*reluctantly*) Well, if she's being honest about that, then no, I guess she didn't really do it.

JETT: So, Sherlock, it wasn't the butler after all.

CARA: I just wish I knew who it was.

13

Scene 2

Scene: LISA'S *backyard*

LISA *is hanging up laundry when* **ANGEL** *walks up the driveway.*

ANGEL: Hi, Lisa. Can we talk?

LISA: Sure.

ANGEL: I just wanted to ask if your friends thought I took your swimsuits. It's just ... they're not very friendly to me.

LISA: (*apologetic*) Well, yeah, we did kind of think that. I'm really sorry. We don't think so anymore.

ANGEL: (*relieved*) Good. (*pointing excitedly*) Oh, look, Lisa—there's the cat!

They watch the stray cat come over to the washing basket, take out Lisa's swimsuit, and drag it away.

LISA: My swimsuit!

They follow the cat to the garden shed and look inside.

ANGEL: All your swimsuits!

LISA: Of course! That first time it went missing, I had left my swim bag outside while I went back inside to get my homework. Angel must have—I mean, the cat must have taken it then. It never even made it to the changing room at school.

14

ANGEL: You call the cat Angel?

LISA nods sheepishly, and **ANGEL** bursts out laughing.

LISA: What's so funny?

ANGEL: I like that. Guess what I've been calling her?

LISA shrugs.

ANGEL: Lisa!

LISA: (with a wry smile) Because she wasn't very friendly?

ANGEL: Yeah, but I guess I can't call her that anymore. I love cats, but Dad's allergic. I'm sorry I've been kind of hanging around your place, but I wanted to play with the cat, and I thought you didn't want to be friends.

LISA: Well, I'm glad both the Lisas are being friendly to you now.

They laugh.

LISA: And feel free to come see either of us whenever.

ANGEL: We'll have to try to stop her from stealing your swimsuits, though.

LISA: I think we'll work something out.

She gives **ANGEL** a high five and smiles.

LISA: Sometimes Lisas do the right thing.

Respond to Reading

Summarize

Use important details from *The Missing Swimsuit* to summarize the challenges Lisa faced. Information from your graphic organizer may help you.

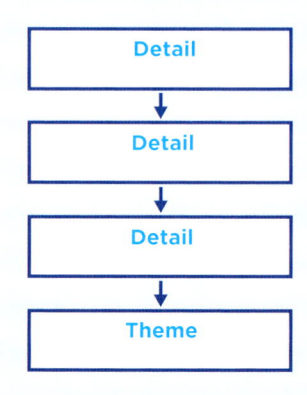

Detail
↓
Detail
↓
Detail
↓
Theme

Text Evidence

1. How can you tell that *The Missing Swimsuit* is a play? **GENRE**

2. What is the theme of *The Missing Swimsuit*? Give several details from the text that support your answer. **THEME**

3. When the dialogue is spoken aloud, the audience might confuse *wear* on page 7 with *where* on page 10. How could the audience use context clues to understand the meaning of each word? **HOMOPHONES**

4. Write about how the dialogue between Lisa and her mother on page 12 helps to convey the theme of the play. **WRITE ABOUT READING**

CCSS Genre Expository Text

Compare Texts
Read on to find out how plays are similar to movies.

MOVIES: PLAYS ON FILM?

Stage theater, or plays, started in Greece in the sixth century B.C.E. Movies, of course, were created much later, in the late 1800s. Despite beginning many years apart, they have many similarities. For instance, they are both usually divided up into three acts, or major sections.

Act 1: The Story Begins. This act introduces the main character and other important characters. It usually also sets up the main character's problem or goal, such as solving a mystery or winning a competition.

Act 2: The Main Action. The second act shows the main character trying to solve the problem set up in Act 1. He or she usually runs into many difficulties that cause things to get worse and worse.

Act 3: The Ending. In the third act, the main character either gets what he or she wants (if it is a happy ending) or does not (if it is a tragic ending).

Greek theater was performed on a stage outdoors.

Both plays and movies use dialogue, sets, body language, and costumes to help the audience become familiar with the characters. In plays, the actors often use exaggerated movements and facial expressions so that the whole audience—even the people at the back of the theater—can understand what is happening. In movies, the camera can film the actors up close. This means that their performances can be more subtle.

Some Early Movie Firsts

1889 — William Dickson, working for Thomas Edison, builds the first motion-picture camera; he names it the Kinetograph.

1903 — Thomas Edison produces the first full-length silent movie, *The Great Train Robbery*.

1905 — The first American movie theater opens in Pittsburgh.

1914 — Winsor McCay releases *Gertie the Dinosaur*, generally considered the first important animated cartoon.

1927 — *The Jazz Singer*, the first full-length movie with both music and dialogue, is released.

1928 — The first Mickey Mouse cartoon, *Steamboat Willie*, is released. It is one of the first cartoons with sound.

1937 — Walt Disney releases his first full-length animated movie, *Snow White and the Seven Dwarfs*, and it is hugely successful.

Another difference between plays and movies is that plays are limited by what they can show in a small space. Because of this, each scene usually takes place in a single location. Films, however, can show a variety of settings and use computer-generated special effects. They can delight an audience by showing actors doing things that they could not do in real life. But plays also have benefits that films do not. There is a special kind of energy between actors and a live audience. This can make plays very exciting to watch.

Although they use many different techniques, plays and movies have a shared purpose. They are both forms of visual storytelling. Whether told on a stage or on a screen, the stories are brought to life for the audience's enjoyment. No matter how much the technology changes, this essential truth stays the same.

Make Connections

In which part of a play do you often find out about difficult decisions the characters need to make?
ESSENTIAL QUESTION

How well does *The Missing Swimsuit* conform to the structure described in *Movies: Plays on Film*? **TEXT TO TEXT**

19

Focus on Genre

Drama Drama refers to plays, films, puppet shows, and other forms of performance in which actors pretend to be characters and act out a story. An opera is a drama set to music. Plays have a written form, or script, that shows the actors what to say and where, when, and how to say it.

Read and Find Play scripts have features that make it easy for the actors, director, and stagehands to perform the drama. Stagehands work behind the scenes to shift props. Movies have scripts, too, as well as other supports such as storyboards, which show what each scene should look like.

Your Turn

Work with a small group to design a set, such as a painted backdrop, for one scene of *The Missing Swimsuit*.

Use the stage directions in the play to guide you. How might you show a swimming pool on stage?

Draw sketches of the scene and of every character.

Present and explain your sketches to the class. If possible, perform the scene for your class.